Let's Discuss

RACISM

Jon Mayled

KU-308-606

909-308-606

Let's Discuss

Let's Discuss Animal Rights
Let's Discuss Drinking
Let's Discuss Drugs
Let's Discuss the Media
Let's Discuss Pop Music
Let's Discuss Poverty

Let's Discuss Racism
Let's Discuss Religion
Let's Discuss Sex
Let's Discuss Smoking
Let's Discuss Unemployment
Let's Discuss Violence

The case studies in this book are fictitious. They are not subject to copyright and may be reproduced for use in the classroom.

First published in 1986 by
Wayland (Publishers) Ltd
61 Western Road, Hove
East Sussex BN3 1JD, England

British Library Cataloguing in Publication Data
Mayled, Jon
    Let's discuss racism.——(Let's discuss)
    1. Racism
    I. Title
    305.8   HT1521

ISBN 0–85078–866–8

© Copyright 1986
Wayland (Publishers) Ltd

Typeset, printed and bound
in the UK at
The Bath Press, Avon

89686

301. 451 M

Front cover: A demonstration protesting against police harassment of Blacks in London, 1985.

Contents

Introduction

This book is about racism. The difficulty in writing a book like this is that although we can try to see the question from other people's viewpoints, we are born into a particular group, and this must affect our outlook.

I am English and white, so this of course influences my thoughts and opinions. Although I shall try to show the problems surrounding the question of racism as they affect black people in this country, I am writing about this as a white person. I have no right to speak as a black person or to pretend that I can speak on behalf of black people; I would not want to give that impression.

Black people are the victims of racism, but it is something which white people have the greatest responsibility to fight and remove.

What Is Race?

If you look up the word 'race' in a dictionary, you will find a definition like this one in the *Collins English Dictionary:*

> 'A group of people of common ancestry, distinguished from others by physical characteristics, such as hair type, colour of eyes and skin, stature etc. Principal races are Caucasoid, Mongoloid, and Negroid.'

But what does this actually tell us? It seems to suggest that a race of people is a group that can be identified in some way. The same dictionary will tell you that a Caucasian is a 'white man' and that Mongoloids have yellowish complexions and straight black hair.

We might then think that an easy way to distinguish between races is by physical appearance. Therefore, looking around the towns and cities of Britain, we should be able to categorize people by the colour of their skin, the shape of their eyes, or other physical features.

We have a problem, however, when we realize that there are many Jews in Britain and that unless they are members of very orthodox sects, and so dress accordingly, they look just like any other white-skinned people.

Opposite: *Two young Jewish men in London. If it were not for their yarmulkahs (caps), it would be difficult to place them racially.*

4

NORFOLK COLLEGE LIBRARY
KING'S LYNN

On the other hand, we could easily pick out everyone who has bright red hair and although we could say that they 'belong' to a group of red-haired people, we would certainly be wrong to call them a race.

We find that it is impossible to identify racial characteristics with any certainty. We can state that *most* Maoris are less than six feet tall or that *most* people with black skin and who come from Africa or are of Afro-Caribbean descent have a certain type of hair. These are essentially true statements, but they tell us only about the physical appearance of these people. They tell us nothing else. The fact that people do come from different races does not give rise to racism; it is the use of those differences to assert a false superiority that causes racism.

All over the world there are billions of people. Each one is different and an individual in his or her own right, with individual ideas, beliefs and physical characteristics. Statements such as: 'All Whites are lazy' (or 'stupid' or 'greedy' or 'smelly') ignore this difference between individuals. Comments of this sort are not only unkind and untrue, but also lead to stereotyping and

These children do not see each other in terms of race, but as individuals. However, that is all too likely to change as they grow older.

Racial stereotyping may easily result in persecution and conflict.

prejudice. The people saying them are ignorant and foolish. The fact that many people believe these generalizations shows just how widespread and dangerous racism is.

Although we have seen that the whole idea of race is vague and unsatisfactory, we are going to need a way of describing people who live in this country and whose families originally came from such places as Africa, the West Indies, eastern Asia, India and Pakistan. I shall use the word 'black' because it is chosen by many of these people to describe themselves. It is a general term, not a description of colour. It is not intended to cause offence to people who do not consider themselves black-skinned.

1 Why do you think people make statements beginning 'All Blacks are...'?

2 What problems arise as a result of looking at people in terms of their race or their physical characteristics?

3 Is your view of other people influenced by the colour of their skin?

Discuss the following statement: 'It is not possible to make any general statements about the appearance of the members of a certain race.'

What Is Racism?

The word 'racism' is used when people or institutions discriminate against other people because of the colour of their skin or because of the race to which they belong. It also involves power: racists discriminate against their victims from positions of social and economic power over them. As you read this book, you will see that almost every aspect of our life in this country is affected by racism. This racism can take many forms: from actual physical attacks on black people to discrimination against them in housing and education, and from laws made to prevent their families joining them in this country to racist name-calling, graffiti and jokes.

The National Front and the British Movement are both organizations which think that only white Anglo-Saxons should live in England and that everyone else should be forced to leave and go back to the country where their racial group 'belongs'. Besides being overtly racist, these organizations fail to take into account that many members of the so-called 'immigrant population' were born in this country. Figures released by the Office of Population Censuses and Surveys show that in 1981, 37 per cent of Britain's Blacks had been born here. This is as much their home as a white person's, a fact that racist organizations choose to ignore.

Racism is not a problem confined to Britain. This picture shows a meeting of the Ku Klux Klan, an American organization which for more than a hundred years has committed violence against Blacks.

Racial prejudice is often based on such innocuous things as the clothes people wear or the food they eat.

If we go on to consider why people are racist, there are two main reasons which we might give in answer. The first is very much to do with how people think. When young children are given something to eat which they have never seen or smelt before, they often refuse the food. It is strange to them and they may well say that it is 'nasty'. They have no way of knowing whether it is unpleasant or not, but because it is unfamiliar, they are frightened of it. As they get older, most people grow out of these childish ideas, but some of them never do.

In many ways we can say exactly the same thing about our reactions to people who look different from us or speak differently from us.

We may laugh when a child is frightened by strange food, but there is nothing funny about an ignorant adult who is a racist. A report conducted

9

by the Commission for Racial Equality into the housing policies of Walsall Metropolitan Borough Council between 1978 and 1981 recorded the following statement made by one council tenant:

> 'On the whole Asians will not conform to our way of life and the way things are going in (these) flats they are going to be turned into ghettoes.'

Statements like this one are often made to justify racial discrimination, but all they reveal is the way in which some people react irrationally through their own fear and ignorance of others.

The reasons why institutions such as governments are racist tend to be different. In these cases, racism is far more likely to be motivated by greed and economic and political advantage. About 400 years ago, several European countries such as France, Spain, Portugal, the Netherlands and England sent merchants to trade with countries all over the world and especially with Africa, India and the West and East Indies. At first the merchants traded on an equal basis with the inhabitants of these countries, but greed soon took over. The Europeans realized that with their navies and gun power they could take what they wanted, instead of paying for it. They also took the inhabitants of these countries as slaves.

Racial hatred: a Nazi swastika and the words 'Juden Raus' ('Jews Out') daubed outside a synagogue in Leeds.

An illustration of slaves from Africa being bought and sold by white traders in Charleston, in the American South.

As early as 1619, Africans were being taken to America as slaves. They were forced to work on the cotton and sugar plantations of the southern states of America and the West Indies. Over the next 200 years, it has been estimated that somewhere between 15 million and 60 million (some estimates go as high as 150 million) Africans were placed in slavery. About two-thirds of these slaves died while being transported across the Atlantic. Slavery did not of course just come into existence with the growth of the European powers. For many thousands of years, and in many parts of the world, people have taken their conquered opponents as slaves. Not always, however, have they sought to justify their actions in terms of race.

Slavery was abolished in the British Empire in 1833, but even today it still exists in some parts of the world. Moreover, it is a subject which has not ceased to be affected by racism. In most of our teaching about the fight against slavery, the role of black leaders such as Toussaint L'Ouverture, Cudjoe the Marron and Nanni, Queen of the Mountains is ignored and the only person mentioned is the white man, William Wilberforce.

In the nineteenth and twentieth centuries, the European powers completely took over India and Africa, which then became known as colonies. The people there were deprived of the land which their families had owned for hundreds of years and could live only where they were told to by their conquerors, for whom they also had to work. In 1884 the governments of Europe met to decide which parts of Africa they would each own. They believed that they had the right to do this and, in some ways, even considered it a duty. Rudyard Kipling, the poet and author, wrote of the 'White Man's Burden' to serve the world by giving it European values. The colonizers, however, ignored and then largely destroyed the civilized kingdoms of Africa, such as the Ashanti, Benin and Ibo kingdoms.

Many Africans suffer from poverty which in some cases can be traced to the European colonization of the continent.

The wealth of white South Africa is dependent on the oppression of the country's Blacks, sometimes with the use of force.

Most of these colonies have at last been returned to the people to whom they really belong, but there are still exceptions. The most infamous of these is the Republic of South Africa. In that country, Whites account for about 16 per cent of the total population, yet it is they that own most of the land and elect the government. Asians and 'Coloureds' have token representation; Black Africans have none.

Using the policy of apartheid, the South African Government keeps black people separate from the Whites in all areas of life and limits the opportunities open to them. White people are able to have a very high standard of living because Blacks are deliberately kept poor and made to work for them.

Case Study 1:
Heinrich, aged 82

Heinrich Geiger was born in Germany of Jewish parents. He was working in Munich as a solicitor when Adolf Hitler came to power in 1933. Later that year the authorities forced him to stop work: Hitler had ordered that Jews could no longer be doctors, solicitors or newspaper editors.

In 1935 a law was passed which meant that Jews could no longer meet friends who were not Jewish. Hitler and the Nazi Party were determined to remove all Jews from Europe. Heinrich was required to carry an identity card and his passport was stamped with the letter 'J'. He was not allowed to drive his car and he and his wife could only go shopping at certain hours of the day. In November 1938, his local synagogue was looted by the Nazis. Nearly all the synagogues in Germany met with the same fate.

In May 1942, Heinrich and his family were ordered to report to the railway station. Together with his wife, their two children and his mother, who was nearly 70, he was bundled into a cattle truck. There were seventy-five people in the truck, with no doctors and no lavatories. They travelled under these disgusting conditions for several days.

Eventually they arrived at a Nazi camp called Auschwitz. Here Heinrich's mother was immediately separated from them and was not seen again. The conditions at Auschwitz were like a nightmare; the Jews were starved and there was no medical help. They were treated by the Nazis as less than human and were used for scientific experiments. After some weeks, Heinrich's wife was taken to the gas chambers and killed. The children died simply by being ignored and left to starve.

Heinrich does not know why, or how, he survived the Nazis. Today he lives comfortably in England, but he has never forgotten the Nazi persecution of the Jews. 'Some people think that we are too sensitive about racism these days,' he says, 'but I don't agree. When you think that 9 million people died as a result of Nazi genocide, you realize just how important the fight against racism is.'

Opposite: *An elderly Jew being surrounded by Nazi soldiers in Berlin, Germany, in 1933.*

1   Why do you think people join organizations such as the National
    Front and the British Movement? To what extent do you think ignor-
    ance is to blame?
2   In what ways do you think people's ideas about slavery have
    changed in the last hundred years?
3   Can you suggest what advantages the Nazi Party hoped to gain
    through the persecution of the Jews?

Consider the following opinion: 'The National Front and the British
Movement should not have the right to hold marches and meetings
and to openly recruit members.'

The Population of Britain

There has always been immigration, and for hundreds of years people have been coming to live in Britain. There have been black communities in the ports of Liverpool and Cardiff for centuries. Indeed, it has often been said that immigration and racial intermingling have been responsible for the rich culture of Britain. It was not until 1905 that Parliament first passed a law which meant that people could be prevented from entering the country; this was done to halt the flow of Jewish refugees who were moving to Britain from eastern Europe.

In a speech made in the House of Lords at the time, Lord Harwicke stated that if immigrants were allowed to continue to become part of the working classes in the cities, 'these classes would become to a great extent non-English in character' and would doubtless fall further 'below our present by no means elevated standards'.

After 1905, other laws were passed making it more and more difficult for people to move to Britain. Nevertheless, as the British Empire came to

Many of Britain's black communities have been established in this country far longer than many racists would have us believe.

Many of the people encouraged to come to Britain in the 1950s and 1960s found themselves in poorly paid jobs which Whites did not want.

an end, many of the former colonies became members of the Commonwealth. Some of the residents of these countries, all of whom were British subjects, then moved to Britain, attracted by the prospect of employment and a higher standard of living.

Following the Second World War, there was a great shortage of labour in Britain. As a result, the government began recruiting workers from Europe; about 90,000 people came to live and work in Britain. However, there were still more jobs than people to fill them, so organizations such as London Transport, the National Health Service and the British Hotels and Restaurants Association began advertising in the West Indies to encourage workers to move to Britain. From the early 1950s onwards, several thousand people a year emigrated from the West Indies in response to the offers made in these advertisements. Until 1958, the number of people migrating to Britain almost exactly matched the demand for workers.

Eventually, increasing unemployment in Britain led to the immigration laws being made tighter, so that it became more difficult for people to move here. Laws designed to prevent and restrict immigration have often been justified in terms of protecting the jobs of people already living in Britain, but figures from the Office of Population Censuses and Surveys show that between 1971 and 1983, 465,000 more people emigrated from Britain than arrived here.

The various ways in which successive British governments have attempted to control the flow of immigration is reflected in figures showing the number of immigrants, by place of origin, moving to Britain in certain given years:*

	1955	1959	1960	1963
West Indies	27,550	16,400	66,300	7,928
India	5,800	2,950	23,750	3,050
Pakistan	1,850	850	25,100	−137

West Indians arriving in Britain in 1962.

Immigration and Race Relations in Britain by Sheila Patterson (OUP & Institute of Race Relations, 1969)

People from Commonwealth countries have found it increasingly difficult to settle in Britain as immigration controls become tighter.

The massive increase of 1960 can to a large extent be attributed to fears that measures to cut back on immigration were about to be introduced. These measures in fact came into operation as a result of the Commonwealth Immigrants Act of 1962, the effects of which can be seen in the immigration statistics for 1963. The argument that the Commonwealth Immigrants Act was designed to protect jobs seems a false one; it was motivated far more by racial prejudice. This view is borne out by the fact that immigrants 'of good type' (i.e. White), as one Cabinet minister put it, continued to enter the country with less difficulty than Blacks.

In the last twenty years, a variety of curbs have been placed on immigration. Critics say that black people suffer most from these measures; Whites, they say, are far more likely to be allowed to settle. The culmination of all this was the British Nationality Act of 1981, which stopped almost all black immigration to Britain, except in cases where people could prove that they already had a job to take up. It has been said this act created different classes of British citizens and meant that for the first time, people born in Britain no longer had British citizenship automatically.

The only people who can move here easily are those from the countries which form the European Economic Community (EEC), and of course most people coming from these European countries are white.

At the time of the 1981 census, the population of Britain was 52,760,331. People from the New Commonwealth and Pakistan made up only 4.2 per cent of the total. Of these, more than half of those people of Caribbean origin and a third of the Asians were born here.

As well as those people who have settled in Britain, there is another group, called 'migrants', who are here to work but have to renew their permission to stay annually. There are about 30,000 Portuguese, 14,000 Filipino and 6,000 Colombian migrants in Britain. There are also many others from Morocco, Turkey and elsewhere.

A Sikh temple in Bradford. As a multiracial society, Britain has a rich variety of customs and cultures.

> *1 Do you accept that controlling immigration is vital to protect the jobs of people in this country?*
> *2 Do you think the fact that a growing percentage of the Black population has been born in Britain will alter racist attitudes?*
>
> *Discuss the following statement: 'People from the EEC should have greater opportunities to settle here than people from the Commonwealth, the countries that were once British colonies.'*

Institutional Racism

Although Britain is a country proud of its traditions of justice and democracy, almost every aspect of life here is infected with racism. Sometimes black people have been able to get things changed, but we need look only at some of the incidents which have taken place over the last few years to see how far this institutional racism goes.

Many black Christians complain that they have been made to feel unwelcome when they have attended British churches. As a result, a large number of Blacks have formed their own independent churches, which Whites may attend if they want to.

One of the most important parts of our lives is where we live. In 1971, the census showed that 4 per cent of white families lived in homes which they shared with another family; the figure for black families was 21 per cent. Blacks are also ten times as likely as Whites to have to share a bath with another family and six times as likely to have to share a toilet. Because more Blacks than Whites are unemployed or in poorly paid jobs, they tend to be forced to live in the worst housing. Moreover, some landlords are not willing to take on black tenants. There is also discrimination against black people on council estates. An investigation was conducted in 1983 into the housing policy of the London Borough of Hackney. The Commission for Racial Equality report found that 79 per cent of all council houses were

Worshippers outside the Church of God in Brixton, London.

given to Whites, whereas Blacks received 54 per cent of all flats. As houses were considered to be more desirable than flats, the investigation concluded that the council was operating a racist system.

Black people are twice as likely to be placed in mental hospitals as white people, and, once there, they are more likely to receive drugs and electric shock treatment than Whites are. Much of the blame for this is to be attributed to the fact that many white doctors do not understand the culture and way of life of black people. In addition, there is the great stress under which many black people are placed by the racism and prejudice they encounter on nearly every day of their lives.

We hear a great deal in the media about riots and fights, often between young people and the police. There were riots in Brixton and Toxteth in 1981 and again in Brixton, Tottenham and Handsworth in 1985. In each case the trouble was reported as being mainly between the police and young Blacks; the fact that white people, too, were involved in rioting and looting is largely ignored. Both white and black people suffer deprivation and poverty in the inner cities, and in the section on employment, you will see something of the problems caused by high unemployment among Britain's young Blacks.

Housing is generally poor in Britain, but in many black areas, residents have to live in virtual slum conditions.

A recent protest against what many Blacks see as a campaign of harassment of their communities by the police.

There have been many reported incidents of the police discriminating against black people, especially during these riots and in the periods leading up to them. The Brixton riots of 1985 were prompted by the accidental shooting by police of an innocent black woman, and the death of another black woman during a police raid was said by many to have set off the Tottenham riot of 1985. In 1981, a report in the *British Journal of Criminology* found that the police were likely to treat Blacks more severely than Whites. Blacks were also more likely to be charged with a crime rather than being referred to a juvenile bureau. Many black people say that the police do not take racist attacks seriously and make little effort to help them.

It also appears that the courts do not treat people equally. In 1981, a report entitled *Ethnic Minorities and Borstal* published by the Home Office showed that in one particular borstal the black inmates had committed fewer crimes than the Whites, and that their crimes were not more serious. The percentage of the black population in prison is far higher than that of Whites.

Talking about racism in Britain, Salman Rushdie, the best-selling author, said:

'Britain is now two entirely different worlds, and the one you inherit is determined by the colour of your skin.'

Such British institutions as the Ascot Races are still predominantly white preserves. Why do you think this is so?

1 Look at the area in which you live. Do Blacks appear to live in the worst housing? If so, what reasons can you give for this?

2 To what extent do you think cultural differences are to blame for instances of Blacks and Whites misunderstanding each other?

Consider the quotation above the picture. Discuss whether Britain really is 'two worlds'.

Racism in Education

Education ought to be the one area of life in which everyone is treated equally and has an equal chance, regardless of their race, religion, sex or the colour of their skin. Unfortunately, this is not the case.

You will see in the section on employment that most black people who are in work have unskilled jobs. This means that the majority of black people in Britain are placed in what is generally known as the working class. The teachers in this country tend to be white and middle class, so working-class children are often at a disadvantage because of this difference in background, and because teachers might not expect them to do well. Black children have the disadvantage of being seen as both black and working-class. One Reading teacher asked about multiracial education compared black children to working-class Whites, saying both showed 'a predisposition to immediate gratification rather than long-term gain'.

If both white and black children are to be treated fairly in schools, it is vital that all racist assumptions about their abilities are discarded.

Many teachers still think that if pupils cannot speak English 'properly', they are unintelligent. Many Asian children speak another language at home and therefore have to learn English as a second language. Some West Indian children speak in a dialect which teachers say is 'incorrect' or 'wrong'. These are extra barriers which black people have to cross in order to succeed.

West Indian children fare worse in examinations than white and Asian children. Research has suggested that this may be partly caused by teachers who believe that children of different racial groups have different abilities. They do not *expect* West Indian children to do well. In 1983, there were about 800 black teachers in Britain out of a total number of over 450,000. Obviously we need more if all children are to be given a fair chance.

An increase in the number of black teachers would prove to children that Blacks can, and do, achieve positions of power and respect.

Learning about different cultures is an increasingly important part of education.

In a report published in 1985 by the Commission for Racial Equality, it appears that some schools are far more likely to suspend black children or send them to special disruptive units, than they are white children for similar behaviour.

For some years many schools have made an attempt to follow a multi-cultural curriculum. It is hoped that this will encourage all pupils to feel that their own race, history and culture are important, and to prevent them being misinformed. Recently, however, black teachers and black parents have pointed out the need for all children to be educated in anti-racism in the hope that real change will begin to take place.

Case Study 2:

Karen, aged 15

Karen's mother was born in Trinidad and her father comes from Barbados. She lives with her mother and three younger sisters in a two-bedroomed council flat in West London. Karen's father has returned to the West Indies, because he had been unemployed for two years. Karen's mother used to be a bus conductor, but because of an accident, she is no longer able to work. This means that Karen, as the oldest daughter, has had to take on much of the responsibility for looking after the family.

Karen had not enjoyed school since the first few weeks she was there, when she was called 'wog' by some of her classmates and 'blackie' by a teacher. 'After a few months, most of the abuse had stopped,' she says. 'I had made friends with some of the other children, both black and white, and those I wasn't friendly with just kept themselves to themselves. Most of the teachers were fair, but some of them seemed to think that they needed to explain everything twice to the black kids. One of them even suggested that I should have elocution lessons.'

When it was time for Karen to choose the subjects which she wanted to study for exams, she found that the careers teacher had already made the choice for her. Apart from the subjects which everyone did, she was going to study dance, drama and cookery. Apparently, the other teachers thought that she was not suitable for their subjects and the PE teacher had said she had 'natural rhythm'. Almost all the members of the dance group were black. The only person who was not asked for an opinion was Karen.

Despite every attempt which she made to explain that she wanted to study science subjects, no one would listen. 'The physics teacher told me that I didn't understand the subject well enough to take an exam in it,' she explains. 'Apparently I didn't have a scientific mind.'

Finally Karen completely lost her temper and threw a chair at her PE teacher. Now she has been expelled from school. She has no exam passes and a bad reference. The headmistress said that she was very sorry that Karen had to leave, but that black children could be very violent and must learn to control their tempers.

Opposite: *Black women face a double barrier to their succeeding in subjects like chemistry.*

1   Consider the remark made by the teacher on page 25. Is this a case of racial stereotyping or is it a comment made in the interest of finding out why black children sometimes do badly at school?
2   Do you think it is important that everyone should speak English in the same way? Do all white English-speakers have similar accents?
3   Why do you think some teachers expect West Indian children to do badly at school?
4   To what extent is Karen to blame and to what extent are her teachers responsible for her situation?

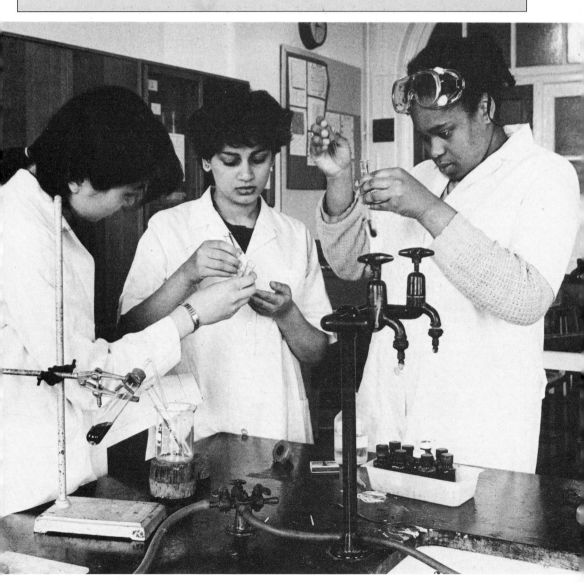

NORFOLK COLLEGE LIBRARY
KING'S LYNN

Racism in Employment

You may think that when you apply for a job the employer will decide whether to give it to you or not by trying to choose the most suitable applicant. If the applicants are all white, then this is quite possibly what will happen; if some of them are black, however, the system may well be different.

The following figures were published in 1977*. They show the number of men, as a percentage of the total number in each racial group, employed in manual and non-manual work.

	Men in manual jobs	Men in non-manual jobs
Pakistanis/Bangladeshis	58%	8%
Indians	36%	20%
West Indians	32%	8%
East African Asians	26%	30%
Whites	18%	40%

Blacks make up a far larger proportion of the unemployed than they do of the overall population. Many of those who do not claim benefit are in poorly paid, insecure jobs.

* Racial Disadvantage in Britain by D. J. Smith (Penguin, 1977)

Black women often face an impossible fight to be taken seriously for other than the most poorly paid jobs.

These figures are for men. Women, who have always had a problem getting properly paid work in this country, have a far greater problem if they are also black. Indeed, very few black women in Britain work in skilled jobs; most of those who are employed have unskilled positions as catering assistants, office cleaners and assembly-line workers, to name a few.

Why, it must be asked, are black men and women not adequately represented in professional work? If they have suffered at school on account of their colour, this will obviously affect their employment prospects. There is also, however, evidence to suggest that direct discrimination by employers is widespread. One personnel manager put it like this: 'I suppose at an interview you tend to look for people who are like yourself. They are not like us.'

Unemployment is continuing to rise in this country, and more and more people are finding it impossible to get work. Although unemployment affects all parts of the population, the percentage of black people out of work is very much higher than that of Whites. When Blacks leave school, their chances of getting a job are four times lower than those of Whites, according to figures from the Department of Employment. In some inner-city areas of Britain, well over 60 per cent of black school-leavers are out of work. Between 1973 and 1975 unemployment doubled, but black unemployment quadrupled. Such figures have prompted some people to believe that in order to have a reasonable chance of getting a job, it is not sufficient to be qualified and able to do the work — you also have to be white.

Very few Blacks are able to gain the opportunity to compete equally with Whites for highly paid, professional jobs.

You might think that the government could make laws to stop this sort of thing happening, and indeed the Race Relations Act of 1976 made it illegal for an employer to discriminate against someone on the grounds of their race or the colour of their skin. Unfortunately, this act has had little effect.

What has happened is that because the law is so difficult to enforce, many people feel it is more useful to carry on looking for a job, rather than to spend time trying to fight discrimination. From 1978 to 1979, only 394 cases were brought before an industrial tribunal under the Race Relations Act. The courts decided that only 58 of these were real cases of discrimination. Even after a case has been proved, the fine which has to be paid by the offending employer is usually so small that it is unlikely to really deter discrimination. More importantly, the person who has been discriminated against is still without a job.

Not only do Blacks suffer most from unemployment, but many of them live in areas where facilities for those out of work are very limited.

33

Case Study 3:

Ranjit, aged 45

Ranjit Patel works in a bakery. There are several Asian men working there, including Ranjit's brother, who got him the job. The men work a 42-hour week, and begin baking at 3.30 am every day. Ranjit and his brother hope that one day they will have managed to save enough money to buy a shop, but most of the money they now earn has to go to their wives and children.

Before coming to Britain, Ranjit had studied at university in Delhi and had spent some time working as an engineer. He had emigrated to Britain in order to be with his brother and mother. As he had brought with him very good references from his employers in Delhi, he believed he would have no problem finding a job. However, this turned out not to be the case. Although he was given several interviews by engineering firms, none of them was successful.

At first Ranjit thought that he was not being offered jobs because other candidates were better qualified or more experienced than himself. Then one day he was sitting at the Job Centre and overheard a phone conversation between the Job Centre clerk and a prospective employer. 'From the way the conversation was going, I thought I must have a good chance,' says Ranjit. 'The employer sounded very impressed by my qualifications, but as the clerk was arranging an interview for me, he mentioned my name. At this point the employer suddenly discovered that he had made a terrible mistake: the post was already filled. A week later I saw it was still being advertised in a local paper.'

Ranjit asked at the Job Centre whether any action could be taken against the employer, but was told that the chances of actually proving a case of discrimination were very small. Ranjit does not mind the hard work and unsociable hours involved at the bakery. 'I want to work,' he says, 'but I do feel that the money and expertise that went into my engineering training are being wasted. The cause of that wastage is racism.'

Opposite: *Many employers have justified racist recruitment policies by saying that they would not take on black employees for fear of upsetting their existing, white workforces. When this fear has been tested, it has usually proved to be unfounded.*

1   From the figures on page 30, you can see that a far higher percentage of Blacks have manual jobs than the percentage of Whites. What reasons can you give for this?
2   It is obvious that racial discrimination in schools will affect the job prospects of Blacks, but in what ways do you think racism in employment affects the schooling of black children?
3   Consider what could be done to improve legal protection for people like Ranjit.

Racism in the Media

The word 'media' is used to describe all the ways in which we obtain information: television, radio, books, newspapers, advertising and so on. For many years the media has been a major influence on the way in which people's opinions are formed. We are all affected by what we see, hear and read, even when we try not to be.

All too often the media prejudices the general public's ideas about black people, particularly through the use of stereotypes. By watching certain television programmes or films, some people may actually be led to believe that Blacks are inferior, stupid people who are to be laughed at. In recent years there have been many programmes about the British Empire in India. In some cases, great care has been taken to ensure that Asian actors are shown behaving normally, and not as ignorant fools. Programmes like this not only avoid racist stereotyping, they often demonstrate the cruelty involved in the British treatment of the Asian population. On the other hand, many of these programmes have simply reproduced the stereotyped ideas held by racist people in Britain. One producer involved in a drama series about India said:

> 'There is no point going into this sort of thing with a 'cowboys and Indians' mentality, as we tended to in the past. Then we used to use English actors in the leading Indian roles, which were at best fairly shallow. That is all changing now, and we are producing better drama as a result.'

Sometimes racist things may seem quite innocent in themselves: an example is the golliwog. This may appear to be just a harmless children's toy, but in effect it creates an image of Blacks which reinforces all the stereotyped ideas about Afro-Caribbean people. The golliwog has a coal-black face and a short fringe of black hair. The lips are red with a white circle around them and the clothes are based on a sort of fancy jacket and pyjama trousers. None of these features are representative of black people. Moreover, golliwogs are associated with the word 'wog', which for a long time has been a word of abuse used to describe black people. Despite all this, golliwogs are still on sale and are still used in advertising. Perhaps the saddest aspect of this is when you see black children playing with golliwogs or wearing golliwog badges. What effect will this have on the way in which those children come to think of themselves and their respect for their colour?

Sometimes black people are used in advertisements, but rarely in a way which will change people's attitudes. Afro-Caribbean actors may be used to sell a product that has the word 'tropical' in it, contains coconut, or is described as 'dark and mysterious'; Asian actors are used as stereotypes

A young Asian boy wearing a 'White Power' badge and T-shirt. The media is to a large extent responsible for the way in which racist attitudes can become acceptable and fashionable, even for their victims.

to advertise curried foods. In each case, black people are shown as peculiar, weird or exotic. They become strange, mysterious and, most importantly of all, *different.*

A peaceful demonstration against the findings of the Stockwell enquiry into the New Cross Fire of 1981.

The media does further harm to the cause of black people in its reporting of news events. In 1981, thirteen black youths were killed in a fire at a party in New Cross, London. Afterwards it was suggested by the parents of these young people that the fire had been started deliberately. Black people from all over the country joined a protest march to complain about the way in which the incident was being investigated. Although some disturbances did take place, the popular newspapers ignored the real issues and chose to report the march with such headlines as 'Day the Blacks Ran Riot in London'. It is this sort of reporting which can do great damage to relations between black and white people.

The media also damages race relations by what is sometimes called the 'invisible Black'. By this we mean instances where black people simply do not appear on television programmes or in books. Over the last few years, we have seen the introduction of some black presenters on television, and both television and radio have begun to produce programmes especially for and about black people. Despite this, the vast majority of books and programmes are by white people, about white people and for white people. Some might say that this is not racist because the programmes and books are not actually representing Blacks in a bad way, but when black people do not appear in the media, the implication is almost that they do not exist. One book publisher asked about the problem stated:

> 'Only one person in twenty-five in Britain is black, yet even now very few areas of our media adequately represent this ratio. Instances of Blacks being shown in a serious, dignified manner are even rarer.'

There are black people living all over Britain and they are a part of everyday life. The picture of life which the media shows is basically untrue. Because of this, many white children continue to believe that Blacks are unimportant and many black children, who do not see other Blacks in positions of respect, lose their motivation and self-belief.

Black and white youths attack a policeman during a riot in Toxteth, Liverpool, in 1981. Most newspapers implied that the riot involved Blacks only.

1 Do you agree that it is more important to have Blacks' producing television programmes than presenting them?

2 Do you think golliwogs should be sold in shops and used in advertising?

3 Consider the statement made by the publisher on page 38. Do you think steps should be taken to ensure that one person in twenty-five in the media is black? In other words, should 'positive action' be taken to counter racism?

Discuss the following statement: 'The media, more than anything else, is responsible for creating racist attitudes in our young.'

Racist Violence

A large number of Britain's Blacks have at one time or another been the victims of racist attacks. Between 1976 and 1981, at least 26 black people were murdered in attacks made on them by racists, and the number of attacks has increased in the last few years. In London alone, the number rose from 840 in 1977 to 1,136 in 1981.

A report entitled 'Ethnic Minorities and Complaints against the Police' conducted by the Home Office Research Unit in 1982 found that there might be as many as 7,000 racist attacks every year. Many acts of violence go unreported by Blacks, because in their experience they have often found the police unwilling to help or believe them. The report also showed that Afro-Caribbean people were thirty-six times more likely to be attacked than white people, while Asians were fifty times more likely to suffer violence.

A Black-owned shop in north London, gutted by a deliberately started fire.

Many communities suffering racist attacks have formed their own self-defence organizations because, they say, the police are unable to protect them.

We might ask why we very rarely hear in the media of instances of Blacks being attacked, whilst if black people are involved in an attack on Whites, the story may well make newspaper headlines. An example of this is the case of the 'Newham Seven', who were sent for trial in 1985. These young Asians were so incensed by the insults and discrimination they had suffered from white people over a period of time that they were finally involved in a fight. They were prosecuted, while the true aggressors, the white racists, were never charged. The trial attracted enormous publicity, as have other similar incidents. This shows the attitude of much of the media and also that of the people for whom it is produced. Newspapers print what people want to read.

Case Study 4:

Jameela, aged 39

Jameela and her husband, Abdul, have moved several times since they came to live in England. They came first to Birmingham in 1972, when the government of General Idi Amin in Uganda forced thousands of Ugandan Asians to leave the country.

They now live in a small flat over a launderette in London's East End. They will have to move again soon, because the owners of the property will not renew their lease. This is because of the damage that has been done to their flat, and to the launderette. All the windows have been smashed in the six months they have lived there. The flat door has been set alight on more than one occasion and excrement has been pushed through the letter box and daubed over the walls. Now the door is covered with the familiar National Front slogans and the walls have been spray-painted with the words 'Pakis go home'.

Every time there is an attack on their property, Abdul and Jameela phone the police, but sometimes they are left helpless. Jameela says: 'About a month ago a gang of youths who had been throwing bottles at the windows managed to break the door down before the police arrived. Abdul had his face cut by broken glass when he tried to stop them coming in. He spent the next three weeks in hospital. While he was away, I went to Birmingham to stay with my sister. I was too scared to stay on my own because gangs of youths are always gathering in our street to cause trouble. I never go out after dark, not even with Abdul.'

The couple's three children are now frightened and confused. Because they are frightened to leave their mother on her own, they say they have stomach ache so they don't have to go to school. Their studies are suffering as a result and they are teased by the other children in their class. 'This of course makes them even more miserable,' says Jameela. 'Although the teachers try to help, there is not much they can do. You can't wipe out a child's experience of years of hatred with just a few kind words. I try to keep the children cheerful, but I don't know how much longer we are going to be able to stay here. We thought we would be able to live in peace when we fled from Uganda, but we haven't had much in the way of peace since coming to England.'

Vandalism against property owned by members of racial minorities is not a new phenomenon, but little has been done to tackle the problem.

1 Can you think of any reasons why the police appear to have been unhelpful to the victims of racist attacks?
2 Are there any measures that could possibly be introduced to stop people being frightened in their own homes?
3 Is there anything Jameela and her husband could do to help themselves?

What Can We Do?

From what you have read, you will realize that there must be changes if people of different races and cultures are to be able to live together in Britain, or anywhere else in the world.

Everyone, whoever they are and to whatever racial or religious group they belong, must have equal rights and equal opportunities to live their lives fully. People should not be in fear of threats from those who are prejudiced against them, and they must never be in the position of being discriminated against because they come from another country or because their skin is a different colour. The way in which black people have been treated in the world, and in Britain in particular, in the last thirty years shows that such equality is still a long way off.

Often we are told that we must wait for change and that things can only happen gradually. This is because it is so difficult to change the way in which people think. However, this is hard to accept for the people who suffer from the ignorant attitudes of racists. It cannot make them feel very much better to know that in twenty or thirty years time things might improve. We all have the right to be treated like equal human beings now. Racism is an evil which must be destroyed.

So, what can be done? As individuals we cannot change the ideas of the government or of thousands of hardened racists, but we can do some

Chinese New Year celebrations in London. People of all cultures can enjoy such celebrations as a part of a new British culture.

A 'breakdance festival' sponsored by the now disbanded Greater London Council. Such activities go a long way towards breaking down the barriers of racial prejudice.

things ourselves to help the situation. First we can make sure that we never tell jokes which are about people's race or the colour of their skin. These may seem harmless enough, but they are based on age-old assumptions of white superiority. Secondly, we can make sure that whenever we see someone we know do or say something which is racist, we try to show them why it is wrong. Finally we need to look at every television programme we watch and every book or comic we read to see whether it is racist in any way. An awareness of racism is the first step in combatting it.

You cannot change the world, but these actions will go some way towards making sure that it will become a more just place, where eventually all people will be able to live as equals.

People seeking advice on all aspects of racial discrimination should contact the Commission for Racial Equality, whose central office is at Elliot House, 10/12 Allington Street, London SW1E 5EH (tel: 01-828 7022). There are also many local organizations helping to fight racism and sponsoring anti-racist events such as concerts and exhibitions.

---

1 Why do you think black people are unwilling to wait for a change in the way in which they are treated? Do you think they should be more patient?
2 Make a list of the steps which you think should be taken to work towards an end to racism in Britain.

45

Glossary

Afro-Caribbean The term sometimes used to denote Blacks who come from the Caribbean islands of Central America.

Anglo-Saxons The word used to mean Whites of English descent.

Apartheid The official South African policy of keeping different races apart, which results in Blacks having the worst jobs, housing, education and land.

Borstal A type of prison for young offenders.

Caricature An inaccurate picture or description of someone that exaggerates certain characteristics they are believed to have.

Citizenship The right to be a member of a given country and to live there permanently.

Colony A country taken over and ruled by people from somewhere else.

Coloureds The South African term for people of mixed black and white descent.

Commission for Racial Equality An organization that seeks to fight racism and to educate people in the values of a multicultural society.

Curriculum The subjects taught in a school or college.

Deprivation A lack of acceptable standards of housing, education, food, etc.

Discriminate To treat a certain person or group of people in an unfair way.

European Economic Community An organization of mainly western European countries formed to make trade and migration between themselves easier.

Genocide The policy of deliberately exterminating a given racial or national group.

Graffiti Words and drawings scribbled on walls, doors and other surfaces.

Immigrants People who move to and settle in a country in which they were not born; the term is sometimes wrongly extended to mean the descendants of these settlers.

Juvenile bureau A type of court that deals with young offenders.

Maoris The original inhabitants of New Zealand, who lived there long before the arrival of white immigrants.

Migrants People who move temporarily from one area or country to another.

Multicultural Having a wide variety of different cultures and values.

Multiracial Made up of people from different races.

New Commonwealth The countries of the British Commonwealth excluding Australia, New Zealand and Canada, most of whom joined the Commonwealth after the Second World War.

Orthodox Conforming to traditional values, ways of dressing, etc.

Persecution An attack, in words or actions, on other individuals or groups.

Positive action A policy of seeking to help an underprivileged group through ensuring they are fully represented in a given group.

Prejudice A biased attitude towards people of particular races, religions, etc.

Stereotype A standard picture or idea used to represent a race or any other group of people which is over-used and often inaccurate.

Further Reading

Non-fiction:

Asian Women Speak Out by A. Wilson & J. Naish (National Extension College, 1970)

Black and White, compiled by John L. Foster (Wheaton, 1976)

Black Leaders in Southern Africa, ed. C. Saunders (Heinemann, 1979)

Black Settlers in Britain 1555–1958 by Nigel File and Chris Power (Heinemann, 1981)

Britain's Black Population (Heinemann, 1980)

Censoring Reality by Beverley Naidoo (Inner London Education Authority & British Defence and Aid Fund for South Africa, 1985)

Different Worlds by F. Klung & P. Gordon (Runnymede Trust, 1983)

How Europe Underdeveloped Africa by Walter Rodney (Bogle L'Ouverture Publications, 1972)

Our Lives (Inner London Education Authority, 1979)

Race in the News by Eileen Totten and Tony Willard (Wayland, 1983)

A Question of Race by Beverley Birch (Macdonald, 1985)

The Caribbean Experience by Douglas Hall (Heinemann, 1982)

The Experience of Colour, ed. M. Marland (Impact Books, 1970)

The National Front by Martin Walker (Fontana, 1977)

World Studies 8–13 by S. Fisher & D. Hicks (Oliver & Boyd, 1985)

Fiction:

Ah, But Your Land Is So Beautiful by Alan Paton (Penguin, 1983)

A Taste of Honey by S. Delaney (Methuen, 1974)

I Know Why The Caged Bird Sings by Maya Angelou (Virago, 1984)

Long Journey Home by Julius Lester (Longman Knockouts, 1978)

News from Babylon (poetry) ed. James Berry (Chatto & Windus, 1984)

Roll of Thunder, Hear My Cry by Mildred D. Taylor (Penguin, 1980)

The Trouble With Donovan Croft by Bernard Ashley (Penguin 1977)

The Young Warriors by V. S. Reid (Longman, 1979)

To Kill A Mockingbird by Harper Lee (Penguin, 1963)

Underground to Canada by Barbara Smucker (Penguin, 1978)

Acknowledgements

The author would like to thank Berenice Miles and Mike Peters for their help and support in writing this book. Special thanks go to Steve Brown and the members and staff of Fulham Cross Club, to whom this book is dedicated.

The publishers would like to thank the following for providing the photographs in this book: Format Photographers *front cover* (Joanne O'Brien), 5, 17, 21 (Val Wilmer), 6 (Jenny Matthews), 23 (Brenda Prince), 24 (Sheila Gray); Sally & Richard Greenhill 8, 9, 20, 22, 25, 26, 27, 30, 31, 32, 35, 37, 40, 41, 44; Photo Co-op 7, 45 (Chris Boot), 16 (Crispin Hughes), 29 (Vicky White); Popperfoto 11, 13, 33; TOPHAM 10, 12, 14, 18, 38, 39, 43; Wayland Picture Library 19.

Index